Visits to Jesus and Mary

Saint Alphonsus Liguori
Edited by Father Joseph Nolen, C.Ss.R.

Excerpted from
*Visits to the Most Blessed Sacrament
and the Blessed Virgin Mary*

Liguori
ONE LIGUORI DRIVE
LIGUORI MO 63057-9999

Imprimi Potest:
Thomas D. Picton, C.Ss.R.
Provincial, Denver Province
The Redemptorists

Imprimatur:
Most Reverend Robert J. Hermann
Auxiliary Bishop
Archdiocese of St. Louis

ISBN 0-7648-1443-5
© 2006, Liguori Publications
Printed in the United States of America
06 07 08 09 10 5 4 3 2 1

This pamphlet is excerpted from *Visits to the Most Blessed Sacrament and the Blessed Virgin Mary*, Liguori Publications, 1990 and 1994.

Liguori Publications, a nonprofit corporation, is an apostolate of the Redemptorists. To learn more about the Redemptorists, visit Redemptorists.com.

To order, call 800-325-9521
www.liguori.org

FOREWORD

Saint Alphonsus de Liguori, the founder of the Redemptorist Congregation, wrote *Visits to the Most Blessed Sacrament and the Blessed Virgin Mary* in the year 1745. The *Visits* have been translated into many languages and used by many people over the years. This abridged version can be used for those shorter visits to the Blessed Sacrament and the Virgin Mary that one makes during the day.

JOSEPH NOLEN, C.SS.R.
LIGUORI PUBLICATIONS

DAILY PRAYERS

Introductory Prayer

(To be said before each visit to Jesus)

My Lord Jesus Christ, I believe that you are really here in this sacrament. Night and day you remain here, compassionate and loving, welcoming everyone who comes to visit you. I adore you and thank you for all the wonderful graces you have given me. I thank you especially for giving me yourself in this sacrament, for asking your own mother to mother me, and for calling me here to talk to you. I am here before you today to thank you for these precious gifts, to make up for all the disrespect you receive in this sacrament from those who offend you, and to adore you everywhere in the world where you are present in this living bread but are left abandoned and unloved. I give you my will, my love, my desires, everything I own. From now on, do what you please with me. I ask only that you love me and keep me faithful to the end of my life. I ask for the grace to do your will exactly as you want it done. My Savior, I unite my love to the love of your divine heart, and I offer them both together to your Father. I beg him to accept this offering in your name. Amen.

Spiritual Communion
(To be said after each visit to Jesus)

My Jesus, I believe you are really here in the Blessed Sacrament. I love you more than anything in the world, and I hunger to receive you. But since I cannot receive Communion at this moment, feed my soul at least spiritually. I unite myself to you now as I do when I actually receive you. Never let me drift away from you.

Concluding Prayer
(To be said after each visit to Mary)

Most holy immaculate virgin and my Mother Mary, I have come to you who are the mother of my Lord, the queen of the world, the advocate, the hope, and the refuge of sinners. I am a sinner, but I give you my most humble homage. I thank you for all the graces you have given me until now, particularly for having delivered me from hell, which I have so often deserved. I love you, most amiable lady; and for the love which I bear you, I promise to serve you always and to do all in my power to make others also love you. I place in you all my hopes; I confide my salvation to your care. Take me under your mantle, Mother of Mercy. Since you are so powerful with God, obtain for me the strength to triumph over all temptations until death. Please give me a perfect love for Jesus Christ and the grace to die a good death. O my Mother, by the love which you bear to God, I beg you to help me at all times, but especially at the last moment of my life. Stay with me until you see me safe in heaven, blessing you and singing your mercies for all eternity. Amen.

FIRST VISIT

Introductory Prayer, page 5

Visit to Jesus

Jesus, you are my life, my hope, my treasure, my soul's only love. Come into my heart, Lord, and stay there forever. You alone must guide my life. Make me desire only to please you and visit you in this sacrament. Make me crave the delight of receiving your Body and Blood. All I care about is your love. Let me forget myself and keep you ever before my mind. Amen.

Spiritual Communion, page 6

Visit to Mary

We have another fountain to drink from—our mother, Mary. Mary was literally filled with grace, as the angel said when he greeted her. God filled her with such tremendous riches so that she could share them with her children. Cause of our joy, pray for us!

Concluding Prayer, page 6

SECOND VISIT

Introductory Prayer, page 5

Visit to Jesus

My Jesus, you are here in the tabernacle precisely to listen to those who come to tell you their troubles and to ask you for help. My heart is heavy as I kneel here before you because I am a sinner. I have seen how good and kind you are, and I have fallen in love with you. I want to love you and please you, but I am weak. I need help. Great Lord, change my selfishness into genuine love. Help me to love you with all my heart. Make my love as selfless as my sins have been selfish. My Jesus, I love you more than anything else in the world. I love you even more than my own life.

Spiritual Communion, page 6

Visit to Mary

Let us confidently approach God's throne, the source of grace, to obtain mercy and find grace to help us when we need it. My Queen, I know you want to help sinners. Look at me: I am a sinner who turns to you. Refuge of sinners, please help me!

Concluding Prayer, page 6

THIRD VISIT

Introductory Prayer, page 5
Visit to Jesus

Here I am, Lord, kneeling before this altar. You are the fountain of grace, the healer of the sick, the helper of the helpless. Have mercy on a sick and helpless sinner. I adore you. I thank you. I love you. Please listen as I plead with you: Give me the courage and the strength to love you. Lord, I love you from the depths of my soul. I love you with all the love I own. Help me to put meaning into those words. Mary, my Mother, my patron saints, angels in heaven, help me to love my God.

Spiritual Communion, page 6

Visit to Mary

Her chains are saving chains. Blessed Lady, keep drawing us to yourself by that chain of trust and love, O kind, O loving, O sweet virgin Mary!

Concluding Prayer, page 6

FOURTH VISIT

Introductory Prayer, page 5

Visit to Jesus

My Savior, you rescued me from my sins by your painful death on the cross. You paid for me in blood, and you keep fresh that sacrifice in every Mass. Do not let all this love go to waste: I put myself at your service. Use me as you please. No longer will I live to please myself, but only to satisfy you. Detach from my soul whatever displeases you. Let me live with the single thought of pleasing you. My God, I love you with all my heart because you desire it and you deserve it. I only wish I could love you as you really deserve. O Lord, make my wish come true. Give me your love!

Spiritual Communion, page 6

Visit to Mary

I am the Mother of gracious love. These words of holy Scripture are applied to Mary, whose love makes souls so beautiful. Mary is a gentle mother who gives away the sweet liquid of divine love. Let us ask our gentle mother for it. O my Mother, help me to give myself completely to Jesus.

Concluding Prayer, page 6

FIFTH VISIT

Introductory Prayer, page 5

Visit to Jesus

Lord, give us the strength to love you intensely. Draw us gently to your love. Make us see the great claim you have on our affection. I love you, my Jesus. You alone are my treasure; you alone can satisfy me; you alone are my love. You have spent yourself lavishly for me. Now I must live my life for you.

Spiritual Communion, page 6

Visit to Mary

My Lady, Saint Bernard says that you ravish hearts, that you steal them by your sweetness and kindness. Take my heart, too, my Queen—I give it to you. Lay it before God with your own. Mother of Love, pray for me!

Concluding Prayer, page 6

SIXTH VISIT

Introductory Prayer, page 5

Visit to Jesus

O hidden Christ, you remain night and day in your tabernacle prison with undying love! Inspire me to think of you, love you, search for you, trust in you alone. Lord, I want to live to love you. My life is worthless if I do not use it for that. And what is there to love but you, who are so good, so kind, so lovable? May my soul expand with love when it thinks of you. And when it hears the names *crib, cross,* and *sacrament,* may it be sparked with the desire to do great things for you. O Lord, let me do something for you before I die!

Spiritual Communion, page 6

Visit to Mary

Let us pray with Saint Bernard: "Remember, my Mother, it is unheard of that anyone trusting in your help has ever been abandoned." O holy Queen, I know that you will not abandon me. Give me the grace to call on you always.

Concluding Prayer, page 6

SEVENTH VISIT

Introductory Prayer, page 5

Visit to Jesus

My lovable Savior, I have come to visit you to show my love. But when you visit my soul in holy Communion you become my food; you become one with me. My Lord, listen to the plea of a soul who is thirsting to love you. I want to love you with all my strength. I want to obey your every wish without self-interest, consolation, reward. I want to serve only to love, only to satisfy, only to please your loving heart. Loving you will be reward enough. Take my freedom, take my will, take everything I own, take my whole being— but give me yourself. I love you, I long for you, I hunger for you, I yearn for you. O my Jesus, make me all your own.

Spiritual Communion, page 6

Visit to Mary

O loving Lady, we call you our hope. You are the hope of all; be mine also. "The whole reason for my hope," Saint Bernard called you. He urges those about to despair to put their trust in you. My Mother, do not let me give in to despair. I place my trust in you. O Mother of God, pray to Jesus for me.

Concluding Prayer, page 6

EIGHTH VISIT

Introductory Prayer, page 5

Visit to Jesus

A God-Man present in this sacrament for me. What a comfort! What a privilege to know that I kneel before God. And to think that this God loves me! Lovers of God, wherever you are, love him for me too. Mary, my Mother, help me to love him. And you, my lovable Lord, become the goal of my heart's desires. Become the sole owner of my will. Possess me completely. I offer you my mind; may it think only of how good you are. I offer you my body; may it always please you. I offer you my soul; may it be yours forever.

Spiritual Communion, page 6

Visit to Mary

Mother of my Soul, no one outside of God desires my salvation more than you do. Show me that you are really my mother.

Concluding Prayer, page 6

NINTH VISIT

Introductory Prayer, page 5

Visit to Jesus

My God, I realize that you deserve to be loved more than anything else in the world. I want to love you as profoundly as the human heart can love. I am not worthy to kneel here before you. I offer myself to you; I love you. Only you can cultivate my barren heart. Change me, Lord! By ignoring you, I have been extremely ungrateful. I haven't the nerve to ignore you any longer. Your boundless goodness deserves boundless love. Starting right now, let me make up for all the love I have held back in the past. My God, I am really serious about wanting to love you.

Spiritual Communion, page 6

Visit to Mary

Mary is like Jesus in many ways. Because she is the mother of mercy, she is glad to help and comfort stumbling sinners. In fact, she is so eager to fill souls with choice graces that a holy man once said, "This Mother is more anxious to help us with her graces than we are anxious to receive them." O Mary, you are our hope!

Concluding Prayer, page 6

TENTH VISIT

Introductory Prayer, page 5

Visit to Jesus

"People are foolish," says Saint Augustine, "when they seek satisfaction in worldly things." He urges them to come to Christ, who alone can satisfy the craving of their hearts. My soul, don't be a fool; yearn only for God. It is easy to find him, for he is close by in the tabernacle. Tell him your needs. He is here precisely to comfort you and listen to you.

Not just anybody is allowed to talk to an important person, says Saint Teresa. Perhaps the closest contact will be through a secretary. But there are no go-betweens when we talk to you, my Lord. In this sacrament you do not stand on your dignity; you are never too busy for anyone. We need only present our problems to find a ready listener. And even if a person finally does get an interview with an important person, how much red tape is involved. Busy people are stingy with their time. But you receive us night and day at our convenience.

O divine Lover, you are an expert at stealing hearts with your love. I want to love you humbly. I submit my will entirely to your will—a will so good, so gentle, so lovable. My God, give me the courage to live for you alone, to love what you love. Let me die for you as you died for me. I deeply regret the times I have so selfishly ignored you. O will of God, I love you because you are one with God. I put myself at your command. You are my love!

Spiritual Communion, page 6

Visit to Mary

My Mother and my Hope, you can make me a saint. I depend on you for this grace.

Concluding Prayer, page 6

ELEVENTH VISIT

Introductory Prayer, page 5

Visit to Jesus

My Redeemer-Shepherd, here I am close to you in this sacrament. The only gift I want is a burning and lasting love for you. Thank you, my faith, for assuring me that what looks like bread in the tabernacle is really my Lord Jesus Christ. And that he is there because he loves me! My Lord, my Everything, I believe you are really present in this sacrament. Take charge of my soul, Lord. I lay it before you and beg you to become master of it forever. I want my will, my senses, and my talents to be subject to your love. I want to use them only to give you pleasure and glory.

Spiritual Communion, page 6

Visit to Mary

Happy is the man who watches at my gate and waits at my doorstep. The poor man begs for a gift at the rich man's gate. That was your life, sweet Mother of Jesus. Help me, teach me to live like you did: happy because you belonged to God. My Hope, help me!

Concluding Prayer, page 6

TWELFTH VISIT

Introductory Prayer, page 5

Visit to Jesus

My Lord and my God, you promised that you will love those who love you, that you will even come and make your home within them forever. I love you, Lord. I love you more than anything in the world. Love me in return. I beg you because I value your love more than all the world's treasures. Come, make your home in my soul. Plant yourself firmly so that you will never have to leave. This is what I live for, my Jesus. Make me love you always. I know you will always love me in return. May our friendship never end!

Spiritual Communion, page 6

Visit to Mary

I promise that I will broadcast your glories in public and in private. O holy Virgin, make me worthy to sing your praises.

Concluding Prayer, page 6

THIRTEENTH VISIT

Introductory Prayer, page 5

Visit to Jesus

My Jesus, I want to please you. I give you my will, I give you my love. You are in this sacrament not only to be near us but also to feed us. Come, my Jesus, come! I desire to receive you within my heart to become the ruler of my will.

I yield everything within me to your love: my delights, my pleasures, my freedom. Lead me, conquer me, rid me completely of whatever is mine and not yours. Let my soul feed on you in holy Communion. Never let it be captivated by creatures that will hold it back from you. I love you alone, my God, and I want to love you forever. Lead me toward you with the chains of love.
Spiritual Communion, page 6

Visit to Mary

O lovable Lady, gracious and gentle, please look after me—a timid soul who trusts you completely. O Mother of God, we run to you for help!
Concluding Prayer, page 6

FOURTEENTH VISIT

Introductory Prayer, page 5

Visit to Jesus

My Lord, I can no longer resist the power of your love. I offer you the rest of my life. I expect you to help me keep faithful to my promise. You loved me even when I turned my back on you. All-powerful God, show the world your might: make me one of your most ardent lovers. Do it through your merits, my Jesus. This is my desire, my resolve for life. You have inspired me with your love; give me the courage to never stop loving you. I thank you for having been so patient with me until now.

Spiritual Communion, page 6

Visit to Mary

My Lady, if you do not help me, I am lost. And if lost, I could never love you in heaven. However, you never abandon those who ask for help. Only those who do not ask are lost. So I turn to you and place all my trust in you. You are the reason for my hope.

Concluding Prayer, page 6

FIFTEENTH VISIT

Introductory Prayer, page 5

Visit to Jesus

My Lord, set me on fire with love for you. Let me think of nothing, crave for nothing, yearn for nothing, search for nothing but you. Make my love for you grow stronger each day of my life. My Jesus, for me you become a victim of love in each eucharistic sacrifice. My Father, I offer you my soul, my will, my life. I unite this small human sacrifice to the tremendous divine sacrifice of your son: his actual death on the cross and its mystical renewal in each sacrifice on our altars. Unite my sacrifice with his. Give me the grace to live up to my offering, Lord, every day of my life. Let me die sacrific-

ing myself for your cause. My Jesus, I want my
death to please you.
Spiritual Communion, page 6

Visit to Mary

My Queen, let me call you what Saint Bernard
calls you: "The reason for my hope." I join Saint
Damascene in saying, "I have placed all my hopes
in you." Inspire me to seek forgiveness of my sins
and perseverance until death.
Concluding Prayer, page 6

SIXTEENTH VISIT
Introductory Prayer, page 5
Visit to Jesus

Lead me to you by the great drawing power of
your love. I would rather be your servant than
master of the whole world. Your love is all I want
from life. What I have I give you, Lord. But even
if the whole universe were mine, I would give

that up in favor of you. Still I renounce what I can: relatives, comforts, pleasures, freedom, even spiritual consolations. I want to give you all my love. I love you more than I love myself, and I hope to love you forever in eternity. My Jesus, I offer myself to you; accept me!

Spiritual Communion, page 6

Visit to Mary

My Lady, you can heal me, and you want to heal me. Here I stand, Doctor of Souls. Heal the cuts and bruises of sin that mark my soul. A single whispered word to your son will heal me. Have pity on me, great Queen!

Concluding Prayer, page 6

SEVENTEENTH VISIT

Introductory Prayer, page 5

Visit to Jesus

My Jesus, I wish I could die defending your presence in the Eucharist. You are there to prove the tenderness of your love. My Lord, since you work so many miracles in this sacrament, I beg you to work one more: persuade me to love you alone. You desire it; you have every claim to it. Give me the courage to love you with all my heart. Give the world's treasures to anyone you please. I reject them all. Your love is all I yearn for and the only thing I beg of you. I love you, my Jesus; make me always love you. I ask nothing more.

Spiritual Communion, page 6

Visit to Mary

Listen to my prayer, O Lady. As a sign that you have, obtain the love I seek from God. Surely he will give it, for he is pleased to see you loved. My lovable Mother, I love you beyond measure.

Concluding Prayer, page 6

EIGHTEENTH VISIT

Introductory Prayer, page 5

Visit to Jesus

My Jesus, you have made your home in this sacrament because you love me. Night and day I would like to kneel at your feet. The angels never leave you because they love you so much. O God, food of angels, divine nourishment, I love you. Help me to drive from my heart every worldly affection that keeps me from loving you alone. I love you from the depths of my soul; I love you with all my heart. If it pleases you, reward this love of mine by making it ever deeper and stronger. Jesus, my Love, give me love!

Spiritual Communion, page 6

Visit to Mary

Here I am, my Mother; I put myself under your care. Be my hope of salvation. Where shall I turn if you reject me?

Concluding Prayer, page 6

NINETEENTH VISIT

Introductory Prayer, page 5

Visit to Jesus

O God, Ocean of Love, you hide your boundless majesty under the form of bread so that you can live close to us. I resolve to visit you often. I want to enjoy your soul-soothing presence—the same presence that brings happiness to heaven's saints. I wish I could kneel here in loving adoration forever. If ever my soul grows lax in its love, if ever it becomes too involved in "getting things done," bring me back to my senses. Inflame me with a burning desire to be near you in this sacrament. If only I had always loved you! If only I had always pleased you! But I still have a chance as long as I am alive. I really want to love you, my Lord, my Treasure, my Love, my Everything. Help me to realize my desire!

Spiritual Communion, page 6

Visit to Mary

I always thank God, my Lady, for having introduced me to you. To ignore you could endanger my salvation. But I love you, my Mother, and trust you so completely that I put my immortal soul into your hands. Happy is the one who trusts in you.

Concluding Prayer, page 6

TWENTIETH VISIT
Introductory Prayer, page 5

Visit to Jesus

My God, wash away every stain and every fault I have committed today. I am sorry for having displeased you. Strengthen me against future falls by inflaming me with an intense desire to love you. My divine Lover, you have made your home in this tabernacle so that I might love you. You have given me a heart that can love profoundly. You deserve my love, and I want you to have it.

Help me to love you, my Jesus! Help me to give you what you really want from me: my heart's profoundest love.

Spiritual Communion, page 6

Visit to Mary

My loving Queen, you are ever ready to help anyone who turns to you. Then I have only to pray to you, and you will listen. Save this poor sinner who now belongs to you. I hope you have understood and heard my plea. Yes, I am sure you have.

Concluding Prayer, page 6

TWENTY-FIRST VISIT

Introductory Prayer, page 5

Visit to Jesus

My sinfulness must make me look like a leper, Lord. Yet you speak to my soul and invite me to come closer. Undiscouraged at the sight of my sinfulness, I approach you confidently. Heal my soul! Dismiss from my heart every affection that keeps me from you, every yearning that you do not want there, every thought that is not directed toward you. My Jesus, I want to please you and to love you alone, because you alone deserve my undivided love. Detach me from everything. Then take me in your arms and hold me so closely that I will never be able to leave you, either in this life or the next.

Spiritual Communion, page 6

Visit to Mary

Great Mother of God, defending criminals who turn to you is your specialty. I plead guilty of offending a God who has favored me with special graces. You can still save me. All you have to do is tell God you will defend my case, and I shall be forgiven and saved. My Mother, you must save me!

Concluding Prayer, page 6

TWENTY-SECOND VISIT

Introductory Prayer, page 5

Visit to Jesus

I marvel at all the measures you have taken to captivate my love. I cannot refuse to love you. I promise that your love shall come before self-interest, self-satisfaction, self-gratification. I will find pleasure in pleasing you, my God. Make me hunger and crave to feed on your body and to keep you company continually. Crush every affection in me that clings to worldly things, Lord. You want my love, my desires, my affections to be directed toward yourself alone. I love you, and I beg for nothing but you. My pleasure is to please you. Accept this desire of a stumbling sinner who really wants to love you. Help me with your powerful graces. Change me from a sinner to a saint.

Spiritual Communion, page 6

Visit to Mary

My gentle Mother, I have disgracefully rebelled against your son. I am sorry for what I have done. I kneel at your feet, hoping you will obtain pardon for me. I am confident that you will supply me with everything I need: courage to ask forgiveness, perseverance, heaven. I hope to praise your mercy forever, my Queen, for having gained heaven through your ministry.

Concluding Prayer, page 6

TWENTY-THIRD VISIT

Introductory Prayer, page 5

Visit to Jesus

Angels in heaven, you adore our God constantly. Fill my heart with the burning fire of your love. My Jesus, open my eyes so I can see how astounding is your love for every single human being. The depth of your love should deepen my love. My Lord, I will love you always, and this alone to please you. I believe in you; I trust in you; I love you; I belong to you.

Spiritual Communion, page 6

Visit to Mary

Lovable Lady, I ask you for help because I know you will listen. No one ever cries out to you without being heard. No one who prays perseveringly to you is ever lost. Only those souls who fail to seek your help eventually find themselves in hell. So if you want me in heaven, my Mother, make me call on you constantly.

Concluding Prayer, page 6

TWENTY-FOURTH VISIT

Introductory Prayer, page 5

Visit to Jesus

My Redeemer, such lavish love leaves me speechless. To show your love for humanity, you veil majesty, you hide glory, you disguise divine life. In the tabernacle you seem to have only one concern: to prove to souls how much you are interested in them. But do souls thank you in return?

O Father in Heaven, accept this feeble love of mine in atonement for the insults inflicted on your son in the Blessed Sacrament. Accept it united to the boundless love that Jesus gave you on the cross and now offers you in this sacrament. My Jesus, I wish I could inspire every human being to love you. Make yourself known and loved!

Spiritual Communion, page 6

Visit to Mary

O rich, wise, loving Queen, you know better than I do what my soul needs. You love me even more than I love myself. I beg you to obtain for me the graces my soul needs the most. Do this and I will be happy. O God, grant me the graces that Mary asks for me!

Concluding Prayer, page 6

TWENTY-FIFTH VISIT

Introductory Prayer, page 5

Visit to Jesus

O divine Heart, engrave on my heart the sufferings you bore so willingly for me. Then when I gaze at them, I will accept and even desire suffering for love of you. Most humble Heart, share your humility with me. O Meekest of Hearts, make my heart meek like yours. Dismiss from my heart everything you do not like. Direct it toward you so that it will yearn for your will alone. Let me live only to obey you, only to love you, only to please you. I know I have a tremendous debt to pay. And even if I wear myself out in your service, I will hardly have begun to pay it. O Heart of Jesus, you are Lord of my heart.

Spiritual Communion, page 6

Visit to Mary

Saint Bernard speaks of Mary as a "lifeboat." She is a lifeboat that will save us from the shipwreck of eternal damnation. Mary, our lifeboat, rescues anyone who calls for help. How unfortunate we would be if we did not have Mary! Good Mother, make us always turn to you for help and encouragement.

Concluding Prayer, page 6

TWENTY-SIXTH VISIT

Introductory Prayer, page 5

Visit to Jesus

O consuming Fire, devour within me every desire for things that distract me from you. I give you my entire self. Starting today, I offer every second of my life to the Blessed Sacrament. Be my comfort and my love in life and at death. In those final moments, please lead me to your kingdom. This is my hope. O my Jesus, when shall I see you face to face?

Spiritual Communion, page 6

Visit to Mary

In you, gentle Mother, we find the cure for our miseries. You have been called "the strength of our weakness." In you we find release from sin's stubborn grasp. My Mother, you are my strength, my escape, my peace, my hope of salvation!

Concluding Prayer, page 6

TWENTY-SEVENTH VISIT

Introductory Prayer, page 5

Visit to Jesus

Eternal Father, I offer you your son. Accept him from me, and through his merits grant me an active and tender love for the Blessed Sacrament. Draw me like a magnet toward the churches where he is present and make me yearn for my next visit to him. My God, give me an all-embracing love for Jesus in the Eucharist!

Spiritual Communion, page 6

Visit to Mary

My Lady, you are my strength. Defend me, fight for me, my Mother. Your name is my safeguard.

Concluding Prayer, page 6

TWENTY-EIGHTH VISIT

Introductory Prayer, page 5

Visit to Jesus

Savior of the World, you are mine if I say but the word. Starting today I consecrate myself to you once and for all: My life is yours for time and eternity. I offer you in sacrifice my will, my thoughts, my actions, my sufferings. Here I am, Lord—I belong to you. No longer will I cling to earthly things that separate me from you. Inflame my heart with divine love. Make me love others only because I see you in them. Eternal Father, I offer you the love that animated the heart of Jesus in his life of sanctity. He has applied his divine merits to my sinfulness. Enrich my soul, then, with the graces he asks for me. His merits have brought me countless blessings. With them I pay off the debt of my sins. Through them I expect from you every grace: forgiveness, perseverance, heaven, and especially the soul-changing grace of your love.

Spiritual Communion, page 6

Visit to Mary

You ease my troubles, comfort me in distress, and strengthen me in temptation whenever I call on you, good Mother. Console me, my Mother. I am loaded with sins, surrounded by temptations, cold in my love for God. Please help me to start a new life—a life that will delight both you and your son. Change me, my Mother; you can do it!

Concluding Prayer, page 6

TWENTY-NINTH VISIT
Introductory Prayer, page 5
Visit to Jesus

Start today, my Lord! I adore you as king of my heart. You are a real lover of souls, a shepherd who loves his sheep too lavishly. Divine Lover, I approach you today with nothing but a hollow heart. I offer it to you so that loving you will be its only occupation. With this heart I can love you and will love you. Capture it; unite it to your will. Let me be like Saint Paul, who said he was in chains for the sake of your love: I, Paul, the prisoner of Jesus Christ. Merge my life with yours, Lord. Teach me to be unselfish—so much so that I would consider myself happy to lose everything, even my life, to be in love with you forever. My Jesus, I love you, I unite myself to you. Let me love you and be united to you always. You alone can satisfy the desires of my heart.

Spiritual Communion, page 6

Visit to Mary

My Queen, you are the one who guides souls to God. Take hold of me, my Mother. Lead a faithless lover like me back to close union with God. You can make me a saint, my Queen, and I depend on you to do it.

Concluding Prayer, page 6

THIRTIETH VISIT

Introductory Prayer, page 5

Visit to Jesus

Divine Heart, you deserve the love of every human heart. O Heart Inflamed With Love, set me on fire with a new life of love and grace. Bind me to yourself so firmly that I will never again separate myself from you. Heart That Shelters Souls, accept me! Heart Crushed by Sin on the Cross, make me really sorry for my sins. I resolve from this moment to please you in every way I can. I will crush human respect and self-indulgence; I will ignore contradictions and renounce all conveniences that keep me from pleasing you perfectly. Lord, give me the courage to love your will. With your overpowering love, smother every other love that is still lingering in my heart.

Spiritual Communion, page 6

Visit to Mary

My Queen, you are rich in love and in your power to intercede. You want every soul to be saved. Help me at every moment. But above all, take me by the hand when you see me staggering from weakness. My Lady, you are my hope, my refuge, my strength; never let me lose the grace of God! In every temptation, I resolve to turn to you immediately with this prayer: Mary, help me!

Concluding Prayer, page 6

THIRTY-FIRST VISIT

Introductory Prayer, page 5

Visit to Jesus

My hidden Lord, with your permission I open my heart to you in full confidence; I want to change, Lord, and I want to amend my life. For the rest of my days I am determined to do everything I can to please you. I love you, my Lord, because you are more lovable than anything else in the world. And in loving you I unite my poor heart to the rich hearts of the seraphim, to the heart of Mary, to the heart of Jesus. My God, I love you from the depths of my soul; let it be that way forever. Amen.

Spiritual Communion, page 6

Visit to Mary

Look at me, my gentle Mother. Count my present sorrows and heed the future dangers that await me. Pray for me. Pray and never stop praying, I beg of you, until you see me safe in heaven.

Concluding Prayer, page 6